lots o' riddles

good clean fun for everyone

CARRIE BROWN

BARBOUR
PUBLISHING

Published by Barbour Publishing, Inc., P.O. Box 719, Uhrichsville, Ohio 44683 www.barbourbooks.com

Our mission is to publish and distribute inspirational products offering exceptional value and biblical encouragement to the masses.

 Member of the
Evangelical Christian
Publishers Association

Printed in the United States of America.
5 4 3 2 1

contents

all in a day's work

Why did the carpenter quit his job?
He was board.

Why are carpenters in charge of building contracts?
They like to hammer out all the details.

How did the carpenter use only one brick to finish building a house?
It was the last one.

What is the rank of a Marine dentist?
Drill Sergeant.

What kind of music do cobblers listen to?
  Sole music.

What is the fastest way to annoy a doctor?
  Take away his patients.

Which water-based profession keeps the best records?
  Fishing. Participants are always dropping a line.

What kind of music do steel workers love?
  Heavy metal.

Why did the pop star smack the Guinness Book repeatedly with a hammer?
  She wanted to produce a hit record.

What's black and white, black and white, black and white?
  A waiter rolling down stairs!

If a gardener has a green thumb and bankers have gold thumbs, who has a black and blue thumb?

A carpenter.

What happened when the nurse took the patient's temperature?

It turned up missing.

Why did the banker sign up for an art class?

He liked to draw interest.

What piece of jewelry do boxers always wear?

A ring.

What kind of people make the best grave diggers?

Excavators who take their job very seriously.

How did the salesman call his client?

He used the sell phone.

Who is in charge of keeping the railroad running?

The track coach.

Why was the car mechanic fired?

He took too many brakes.

What did the Kamikaze instructor say to his students?

"Watch carefully. I'm only going to show you this one time."

How can you tell if the minister is working on his sermon?

See if he is practicing what he preaches.

What did the surgeon say to his patient when he finished the operation?

"That's enough out of you."

How did the carpenter break his teeth?

He chewed his nails.

Why are magicians given hazard pay?
They have to pull their hare out at every show.

If Mr. Green sells cupcakes in his grocery store for 39 cents each, how should he price upside down cakes?
They should be 63 cents each.

Who is the first person in an orchestra to be hit by lightning?
The conductor.

animal kingdom

What animal is impossible to carry on a conversation with?
A goat—he always wants to butt in!

What animal has more lives than a cat?
A frog. He croaks every night!

Why can't you play a joke on a snake?
Because you can't pull their legs!

What animal isn't born with wings, but has the innate ability to fly?
A caterpillar isn't born with wings, but it will fly when it becomes a butterfly.

What is a frog's favorite flower?
 A croakus.

What is the most difficult time to catch a frog?
 In leap year.

What is a frog's favorite game?
 Croak-ay.

What does a frog do when his eyesight goes bad?
 Goes to the hoptician.

Why does the giraffe have such a long neck?
 Because its head is so far from its body.

Why did the otter cross the road?
 To get to the otter side.

What do you say when you see a snail drive past you in a car?
 "Look at that escargot!"

Why is it hard for teenage turtles to be rebellious?

They can never run away from home.

What vegetable do you get when an elephant
walks through your garden?

Squash!

What's black and white, black and white,
black and white, and green?

Three zebras fighting with a pickle.

What did the teddy bear say when he was
offered dessert?

"No thanks, I'm stuffed."

What kept the performing pony from sing-
ing?

It was a little horse.

What does a skunk use to defend itself?

In-stincts.

Why did the weasel cross the road twice?
He was a double crosser.

What has four eyes, one tail, six legs, and two heads?
A person on horseback.

What did the toad say after listening to one of the rabbit's jokes?
"You croak me up!"

What animal rows quickly with four oars but never travels beyond his front door?
A turtle.

What did the zookeeper like to eat for a snack?
Animal crackers.

Why are gophers so busy?
They always have to gopher this and gopher that.

What kind of turtle always has a bad attitude?
A snapping turtle.

How do skunks smell?
With their noses, silly!

What do you call a sick alligator?
An illigator.

What do you call a one hundred-year-old ant?
An antique.

What kind of ant is good at math?
An account-ant.

Where do polar bears like to vacation?
Brrr-muda.

What do you get if you cross a snowman
with an alligator?
Frostbite.

What do you call a grizzly bear with no teeth?
A gummy bear.

How do bears walk around?
With bear feet.

How does a skunk's car run?
On fumes.

What wears a coat all winter and pants in the summer?
A dog.

What happens when a frog's car breaks down?
He gets toad away.

What do you call a group of mice in disguise?
A mousequerade party.

Where do worms like to go for dinner?
Anywhere that is dirt cheap.

Why won't banks allow kangaroos to open accounts?
Their checks always bounce.

What has twelve legs, six eyes, three tails and cannot see?
Three blind mice.

What is the best year for a kangaroo?
Leap year.

How do you keep a skunk from smelling?
Hold its nose.

What animal is the strongest?
A snail. He carries his house.

Where does a skunk sit in church?
In a pew.

What do you call two spiders that just married?
Newlywebs.

What do you get when you cross a rabbit and the World Wide Web?

A hare Net.

What do you get if you cross a parrot with a cat?

A carrot.

What is as big as a hippopotamus, but weighs nothing at all?

The hippo's shadow.

What has keys but can't open locks?

Monkeys, turkeys, and donkeys.

How did the zookeeper catch the escaped cat?

The leopard was spotted.

What dangerous animal did Mrs. Washer have in her backyard?

A clothes lion.

What kind of snake is good at math?
An adder.

What is black and white and red all over?
A blushing zebra.

baby talk

What did the baby corn say to the mommy corn?
"Where is pop-corn?"

What is the best way to put a baby astronaut to bed?
You rock-et.

What snakes do babies like?
Rattlesnakes.

Why do mothers carry their babies?
Because the mothers are too heavy for the babies to carry.

What kind of pen does a baby prefer?
A playpen.

Why did the Army begin drafting babies?
It was trying to build up the infantry.

Why did the baby cross the playground?
To get to the other SLIDE!

Why are babies like old cars?
They always have a rattle.

Why did the baby wear a diaper to the party?
Because he didn't want to be a party pooper!

What do baby geologists like to hear at bedtime?
"Rock-a-Bye, Baby."

Why did the baby King Tut cry?
He wanted his mummy!

What do you call a baby goat when it is sleeping?

A kid-napping.

What can baby lizards do that baby snakes can't?

Learn to walk.

What do you call a baby who eats a lot of beans?

A beanie baby!

When the mommy finished washing the dirty baby, what was still dirty?

The bathtub.

What do babies and basketball players have in common?

They both dribble.

What do baby ghosts wear on their feet?

Boo-ties.

What did the mommy broom say to the baby broom?

"It is time to go to sweep."

birds of a feather

Why wouldn't the duck go to the duck doctor?
Because he was a quack!

Why do birds fly south for the winter?
Because it's too far to walk!

How many penguins does it take to fly an airplane?
None. Penguins can't fly!

What do you get when you put five ducks in a box?
A box of quackers.

What bird can lift the most?
A crane.

What grows down when it grows up?
A goose.

What do you call a big swallow?
A gulp.

What do you call a small swallow?
A sip.

What does a thousand-pound canary say?
"Here, kitty, kitty, kitty."

How do baby birds learn to fly?
They wing it.

Why does a flamingo lift up one leg?
Because if he lifted up both legs it would fall over!

What is an owl's favorite mystery?
A whoo-dunit.

Which bird is always out of breath?
A puffin.

What do you call a penguin in the desert?
Lost.

What kind of dance do woodpeckers excel at?
Tap dance.

What do you call a duck in the NBA?
A slam duck.

Why did the rock band hire a chicken?
They needed the drumsticks.

Why do hummingbirds hum?
They can never remember the words to the song.

What kind of bird shows up at every meal?
A swallow.

What penguin was a famous Antarctic explorer?
Admiral Bird.

When do you have ducks with four feet?
When you have two ducks.

Why shouldn't ducks ever have more than one credit card?
They are only given one bill.

What role did the duck play in the all-animal orchestra?
He was the con-duck-tor.

Why do ostriches have such long legs?
To reach the ground.

brainteasers and mindstumpers

Little Tommy suddenly found himself surrounded by thirty galloping horses, twenty-five charging bears, and ten roaring lions. How did he survive this situation?

He got off the carousel.

A man rode into town on Monday, stayed five days, and then rode out on Monday. How is this possible?

His horse was named Monday.

If a bungalow is red and everything in it is red, what color are the stairs?

Bungalows don't have stairs.

Four cars come to a four way stop, each coming from either North, South, East, or West. It isn't clear who arrived first, so they all go at the same time. No one crashes, but all four cars successfully continue on their way. How is this possible?

They all made right hand turns.

An archeologist found a coin dated 62 BC and immediately declared it a fraud. How did he know it wasn't real?

BC stands for "Before Christ." This dating system wasn't used until after Christ had been born.

Maggie woke up one day with a toothache and went to the only dental practice in town to have it fixed. The dental practice had two partners, Dr. Smith and Dr. Jones. Dr. Smith has a beautiful smile, while Dr. Jones has a mouth of ugly, crooked teeth. Who should Maggie see about the toothache?

Dr. Jones. Since it is the only dental practice in town, Dr. Jones must fix Dr. Smith's teeth and vice versa.

A boat has a ladder that has six rungs. Each rung is one foot apart. The bottom rung is one foot from the water. The tide rises at twelve inches every fifteen minutes. High tide peaks in one hour. When the tide is at its highest, how many rungs are under water?

None. The boat rises with the tide.

A woman says to you "Everything I say to you is a lie." Is she telling you the truth or is she lying?

She's lying. Even though she's lying when she says "everything" she says is a lie, some of the things she says can be a lie, and this is one of them.

Melissa was out shopping one day. She met her father-in-law's only son's mother-in-law. What did Melissa call her?

She called her "Mom."

A baseball team scored four runs in one inning, but not one man reached home. Why not?

It was a girl's team.

If a farmer has five haystacks in one field and four haystacks in the other field, how many haystacks would he have if he combined them all in the center field?

One. If he combined them all, they would become one big haystack.

A woman drove to the video store. She got out, and accidentally locked her keys in the car. She went into the store to rent some videos. She came back out and unlocked the door without touching "anything" on the outside of the car. How did she do it?

The car was a convertible and she reached inside to open the door.

Marco and Anna were sitting in their living room one night. While Marco was watching television, Anna was reading. All of a sudden, the power went out and Marco decided to go to bed. Without the use of a flashlight or candle, Anna kept on reading. How?

Anna was blind. She was reading a book in Braille.

You move to an island in the middle of a lake. This lake is in a remote part of the state and there has never been a bridge connecting the island to the mainland. Every day a tractor and wagon gives rides around the island to tourists. Puzzled as to how the tractor had gotten onto the island, you ask around. You find out that the tractor was not built on the island and was not transported to the island by boat or by air. How did the tractor get to the island?

The owner waited until winter and then drove the tractor over on the frozen lake.

A boy dreamed that a tiger was chasing him through the jungle. As the tiger got closer, the boy came to a tall tree. The boy quickly climbed to the top of the tree, but ran into a large python. Suddenly, he was in danger of being eaten by the snake and the tiger. How did he escape?

He woke up!

What is cut and spread out on the table but never eaten?

A deck of cards.

Jim was three years old at his last birthday and will be five years old at his next birthday. How can that be?

Today is his fourth birthday.

One morning, a man is preparing to leave town, but first stops by his office to pick up his messages. While he is at the office, the night watchman stops him and says, "Sir, don't go on this trip. I had a dream last night that the plane will crash and you will die!" The man decides to cancel his trip. Just as the watchman predicted, the plane crashes and no one survives. The very next morning, the man rewards the watchman with one thousand dollars, but then fires him. Why would he fire the watchman who saved his life?

The "night" watchman was fired for sleeping on the job!

A woman cheered loudly for the winning soccer team's goalie. The woman is the goalie's sister, but the goalie is not the woman's brother. How are they related?

The goalie is the woman's sister.

A man was found murdered on Sunday morning. His wife immediately notified the police. The police questioned the wife and staff and compiled these alibis:

The Wife said she was sleeping.

The Cook was cooking breakfast.

The Maid was gathering vegetables.

The Butler was getting the mail.

The police instantly arrested the murderer. Who did it and how did they know?

> *It was the Butler. He said he was getting the mail, but there is no mail on Sunday!*

A woman shoots her husband. Then she holds him under water for over five minutes. Finally, she hangs him. But one hour later they both go out together and enjoy a wonderful dinner. How is this possible?

> *The woman was a photographer. She shot a picture of her husband, developed it, and hung it up to dry.*

How can the statement "Four is half of five" be true?

> *If four is written in roman numerals (IV) then it is half of f(IV)E.*

A murderer is condemned to death, but he is allowed to choose how he will be executed. The first choice is burnt at the stake, the second is shot by firing squad, and the third is given over to lions that haven't eaten in two years. Which choice is the best?

The third. Lions that haven't eaten in two years are dead.

What gets larger if you take anything away from it?

A hole.

What appears once in every minute, twice in every moment, but not once in a billion years?

The letter M.

Two men wearing packs are found on a mountain. One of the men is dead. The man who survived has his pack open, while the man who was killed has his pack closed. What was in the packs?

Parachutes. The dead man's chute didn't open.

Three men jumped off the Golden Gate Bridge, but one of them didn't get his hair wet. How is this possible?

He didn't have any hair.

Michael and Sophia have the same father and they were born at the same hour of the same day to the same mother in the same hospital. However, they are not twins. How is this possible?

They are two babies in a set of triplets.

A woman has seven children, half of them are boys. How can this be possible?

All the children are boys, so half are boys and so is the other half.

"I guarantee," said the salesman in the pet shop, "that this parrot will repeat every word it hears." A customer bought the bird, but found that the parrot wouldn't speak a single word. However, the salesman didn't lie about the bird. How is this possible?

The parrot was deaf.

What three-word sentence did Adam use when he met Eve for the first time? (Hint: It is read the same forwards and backwards!)

"Madam, I'm Adam."

Linda was making peach jam. She put all the peaches in the pot and began to cook them. Then she remembered she had to add one cup of sugar for every two peaches. How did she figure out how much sugar to put?

She counted the pits.

A horse is tied to a four foot rope, and five feet away is a bail of hay. Without breaking the rope or chewing through it, the horse was able to get to the bail of hay. How is this possible?

The other end of the rope wasn't tied to anything.

If you were running a race, and you passed the person in second place, what place would you be in now?

You would be in second place.

Molly left a solid object on the kitchen counter while she went to play. When she came back four hours later, the object had completely vanished. No one touched it or ate it. What happened?

Molly left an ice cube on the counter.

Ancient Roman magicans used an ingenious method for walking through solid walls. What was it?

A door.

A boy was at a carnival and went to a booth where a man said to the boy, "If I write your exact weight on this piece of paper then you have to give me fifty dollars, but if I can't, I will pay you fifty dollars." The boy looked around and saw no scale so he agrees, thinking no matter what the man writes he'll just say he weighs more or less. In the end the boy ended up paying the man fifty dollars. How did the man win the bet?

The man did exactly as he said he would and wrote "your exact weight" on the paper.

Police found a man hanging in an empty room. There was nothing in the room he could have used to reach the ceiling. All they found when they entered the room was a puddle of water under the dead man. How did he hang himself?

He stood on a block of ice and let it melt.

Once upon a time, there was a clever thief charged with treason against the king and sentenced to die. However, the king decided to be a little merciful and let the thief choose which way he would die. Which way should he choose?

He should choose to die of old age.

A cowboy entered a Wild West bar and asked for a glass of water. The bartender drew a gun and pointed it at the young man. The young man said, "Thank you," and walked out. Why?

He had the hiccups and the bartender scared them out of him.

A man lives on the twenty-fifth floor of an apartment building. On rainy days, he takes the elevator to and from his apartment. However on sunny days, he will take the elevator from his apartment to the lobby, but walks up the twenty-five flights of stairs when he returns home. Why doesn't he just take the elevator all the time?

He's a very short man. On rainy days, he can hit the twenty-fifth button with his umbrella and of course he can always hit the lobby button because it's at the bottom of the console. On sunny days, he doesn't have any way of hitting the twenty-fifth button so he just takes the stairs.

The ping pong ball you are playing with drops into a long skinny hole in the floor. You can't stick your hand down the hole or use a tool to get it out. How can you get the ball without ripping out the floor?

Pour water down the hole. The ping pong ball is light enough to float to the top!

Luke had it before, Paul had it behind. Ladies have it at the beginning. Abraham Lincoln had it twice. Doctor Lowell had it before and behind. He had it twice as bad behind as he did before. What was it?

The letter L.

Christmas and Winter Wonderland

Why do Pilgrim's pants always fall down?
Because they wear their buckles on their hats!

Why wasn't the turkey hungry at Thanksgiving dinner?
He was already stuffed.

What do snowmen have for breakfast?
Frosted flakes.

Why are snowmen so popular?
They're just so cool!

What is King Kong's favorite Christmas carol?
Jungle bells.

What do you call Santa's helpers?
Subordinate clauses.

Who was the smartest wise man?
The one with FrankenSENSE.

What is Rudolph's favorite weather?
Rain!

What do you give a mummy for Christmas?
Wrapping paper!

Who delivers Christmas presents to dogs?
Santa paws!

What did Santa say when his toys misbehaved?
Toys will be toys!

What do you get by putting ice in your father's bed?

A popsicle.

If Santa rode a motorcycle, what kind would it be?

A Holly Davidson.

Which of Santa's reindeer works as a housekeeper during off-season?

Comet; he cleans sinks!

Why didn't Frosty the Snowman get married?

He had cold feet.

Why does Santa Claus go down the chimney on Christmas Eve?

Because it "soots" him!

Which of Santa's reindeers is considered the most ill-mannered?

Rude-olf.

What bites without any teeth?
Frost.

What do Santa's beard and a Christmas tree both have in common?
They both need trimming.

What did Adam say to his wife the day before Christmas?
"It's Christmas, Eve."

What do snowmen wear on their heads?
Ice caps.

What do snowmen eat for lunch?
Icebergers!

Where do snowmen go to dance?
A snowball.

What do elves learn in school?
The Elf-abet.

What mental illness was Santa diagnosed with?
Claustrophobia.

Why did the Christmas cookie go to the doctor?
He was feeling crummy.

What smells everything in a chimney?
Santa's nose.

What do you have in December that you don't have in any other month?
The letter D.

What do you get if you cross Father Christmas with a detective?
Santa Clues.

What is born in winter, dies in summer, and hangs from its roots?
An icicle.

What is Santa's favorite outdoor activity?
Gardening. He loves to ho, ho, ho.

Why was Santa's little helper depressed?
Because he had low elf esteem.

Where do polar bears vote?
The North Poll.

Cops and Robbers

What do polite prisoners say when they bump into someone?
"Pardon me."

Where did the police send the bad gymnasts?
To the parallel bars.

How did the bad gymnasts escape from jail?
The parallel bars were uneven.

Why did the police arrest a twelve-year-old boy while he was playing basketball?
He stole the ball.

What is never requested as a prisoner's last meal?

Minute steak.

What is the best way to search for a giant and a dwarf who have escaped from prison?

Look HIGH and LOW for them.

What was the newspaper headline after ten bottles of expensive French perfume were stolen?

Police dogs are on the SCENT.

How are a lawyer and an escaped prisoner similar?

They both had to pass the bars.

What is an inmate's favorite vegetable?

Cellery.

What cafeteria food do detectives love?

Mystery meat.

Why would a thief steal an entire truckload of soap?
The thief wanted to make a CLEAN getaway!

A truckload of brushes has been stolen.
The police are COMBING the area!

Why is grammer a convict's least favorite subject?
He hates to complete the prison sentence.

What do prisoners use to call each other?
Cell phones.

When the detective got to the crime scene, how did he know that the numbers were guilty?
Their alibi didn't add up.

What did the policeman say to his stomach?
"You're under a-VEST!"

Why did the policeman run across the baseball field?

A player had stolen second base!

How did the detective know that a cat burglar was responsible for the break in?

Missing items included a pussy willow plant and two kits.

Why did the police wake the child?

Because they'd heard there'd been a kid napping!

What is an executioner's favorite paper?

The Daily Noose.

What case did the Private Investigator always doze off on?

The pillow case.

Why was the police officer under the blanket?

Because he was an under cover cop!

What does a policeman fly in?
    A heliCOPPER.

What section of the newspaper do convicts read for kicks?
    The wanted section.

Why did the burglar stop to take a shower?
    He wanted to make a clean getaway!

What is the difference between a jailer and a clockmaker?
    The clockmaker sells watches, and the jailer watches cells.

Why did Lois Lane meet Superman at the ice cream shop?
    She was hoping for a scoop.

Why were outlaws considered the strongest men in the Wild West?
    They were always holding up trains.

Who is the smallest police officer?
The centi-meter maid.

Why did Batman stop at the pet store?
He was looking for a Robin.

Where do the outlaws all live?
In the "Wild" West.

When is a crook neither right handed nor left handed?
When he is underhanded.

What do you call a group of convicts who go to the beach?
A crime wave.

What cowboy wears a black mask just like the Lone Ranger's, rides a horse just like Silver, and has a sidekick who could be Tonto's twin brother?
The Clone Ranger.

What happened to the author at his trial?
The judge threw the book at him.

What type of cases did the literary judge try?
Book cases.

What do you call the police chief's wife?
Mischief.

What is the most common alphabet crime?
J walking.

Why did the police charge the exterminator
with murder?
He was a hired killer.

Why did the FBI agent spray his room with
Raid?
He thought it might be bugged.

down on the farm

Why did the chicken cross the road?
To get to the other side.

Why did the bubble gum cross the road?
It was stuck to the chicken's foot.

Why did the farmer cross the road?
He was trying to catch his chicken.

Why did the rooster cross the road?
It was the chicken's day off.

How does the farmer drive his cattle car?
With a steering wheel.

What has one horn and gives milk?
A milk truck.

What is a common allergy for horses?
Hay fever.

What do you call a goat's beard?
A goatee.

How many legs does a horse have?
Six. It has forelegs in the front and two legs in the back.

Where do cows usually go on dates?
To the moo-vies.

How do you get pigs to write letters?
You give them a pigpen.

Why do cows wear bells?
Their horns don't work!

How did they catch the crooks at the pig farm?

Someone squealed.

What is a pig's favorite play?

Ham-let.

What do you get when you cross a pig and a tree?

A porky pine.

What do you call a sporting event between farmers and railroad conductors?

Track and field.

What should you do if your animals start to stampede?

Hold your horses.

What do you call a cow that has just given birth?

Decalfinated.

What day of the week do chickens fear?
Fry-day.

What do you call a sleeping bull?
A bulldozer.

What do you get from sheep who listen to heavy metal music?
Steel wool.

How can you tell if a pig is angry?
He goes hog wild.

How do you get the attention of a sheep?
Yell, "Hey, ewe!"

What do you call a calf after it's one year old?
Two years old.

How did the farmer fix the hole in his jeans?
With a cabbage patch!

How did the farmer's wife keep track of their farm's steer population?
She used cattle logs.

Why did the chicken fall on the street?
He wanted to take a road trip.

What is the first sign that the corn has a cold?
It develops an earache.

What game do cows like to play?
Scrab-bull.

Why did the stallion collect stamps?
He was a hobby horse.

What farm animal always has a sore throat?
The hoarse.

What side of a chicken has the most feathers?
The outside.

What do you get if you feed gunpowder to a chicken?

An egg-splosion!

What farm animal always wears a wool coat to bed?

The sheep.

What did the corn say when the farmer wanted to talk?

"I'm all ears."

What do you call cattle with a sense of humor?

Laughing stock.

How do you know if a cowgirl is feeling discouraged?

She is at the end of her rope.

When pigs fly, where do they usually sit?

In the cockpit.

What is a donkey's favorite game?
Stable tennis.

How did the farmer repair his broken fence?
He used a cabbage patch.

What is a cow's favorite form of entertainment?
The MOOO-vies!

How did the rancher prepare for each season?
By making long range plans.

Why do chickens like thunderstorms?
They enjoy foul weather.

Where did the sheep go for a hair cut?
To the ba-ba shop.

Where do pigs get their money?
At a piggy bank.

If a rooster laid an egg on the top of a roof, which side of the roof would the egg roll down?

Neither. Roosters don't lay eggs.

Why shouldn't you tell a secret to a pig?

He's a squealer.

What is the largest national use of cowhide?

To cover cows.

How can you know how long cows should be milked?

By watching how the short cows are milked.

What is a sheep's favorite past time?

Base-Baa.

What happened to the cow that survived an earthquake?

He became a milkshake.

easter and spring surprises

How does the Easter Bunny stay fit?
EGGS-ercise and HARE-robics!

What is the best way to find the Easter Bunny?
Eggs (x) mark the spot.

What does the Easter Bunny become after Easter is over?
Tired!

How does the Easter Bunny style his fur?
With hare spray.

What do you get by crossing a parrot and the Easter Bunny?

A rabbit who will tell you where he hid the eggs.

What do fashionable frogs wear in the spring?

Open toad sandals.

Why did the Easter egg hide?

He was a little chicken!

When does Valentine's Day come after Easter?

In the dictionary.

Is it better to write a Valentine's Day note on an empty stomach or a full stomach?

It's better to write it on paper.

Why was Megan so exhausted in April?

She just finished a thirty-one day march!

What's the best way to send a letter to the Easter Bunny?

By hare mail.

Why did the Easter Bunny miss the Easter Parade?

He was busy getting his hare done.

What is the Easter Bunny's favorite kind of music?

Hip-hop!

At what time of year does it rain chimpanzees and spider monkeys?

During the Ape-ril showers.

Why are rabbits so good at math?

They love to multiply.

What did the pink rabbit say to the blue rabbit?

Cheer up!

Why is the Easter Bunny the luckiest animal in the world?
He has four rabbit's feet.

Why does the Easter Bunny have a shiny nose?
His powder puff is on the wrong end!

How does Easter end?
With the letter R.

What do you call a group of Easter bunnies walking backwards?
A receding hare line.

How do you know that carrots are good for your eyes?
Have you ever seen a rabbit with glasses?

What do you get if you pour hot water down a rabbit hole?
Hot cross bunnies!

glass slippers and wooden shoes

Why wasn't Cinderella good at sports?
Because she had a pumpkin as her coach!

How do you get to "Once Upon a Time" land?
You take the fairy boat.

What did the Gingerbread Man use to fasten his vest?
Ginger snaps.

Where do all mermaids like to sleep?
In a waterbed.

What kind of prince did Cinderella hope to find at the beach?

A foot-prince.

What did the Old Woman Who Lived in a Shoe require more than anything else?

A babysitter.

What did Cinderella say while she was waiting for her photos?

"Some day my prints (prince) will come."

What fishing technique do the Three Billy Goats Gruff use?

Trolling.

Why did Cinderella get thrown off the baseball team?

Because she ran away from the ball!

How did the Gingerbread Man make his bed?

With cookie sheets.

What did the little mermaid have at her birthday party?
Fish cakes.

Why was Snow White elected to the Supreme Court?
She was the fairest of them all.

When Sleeping Beauty got lost in the castle gardens, how did she feel?
A-maze-d.

Why was Humpty Dumpty referred to a psychiatrist?
He had cracked up.

What did Cinderella call the cat who helped her get to the ball?
"My furry godmother."

How did Rapunzel find her missing hairbrush?
She combed the land.

What did King Arthur like to sleep in?
A knight gown.

What magic reptile lives in the Emerald City?
The Lizard of Oz.

What color hair did the Wicked Witch of the West have?
Brewnette.

What do The Wicked Witch and The Big Bad Wolf have in common?
The same first name.

What kind of doctor do clock-climbing mice go to?
The Hickory Dickory Doc.

Why wouldn't Cinderella give her prince the time of day?
Because it was midnight.

Why did the dragon sleep all day long?
He planned to hunt the knight.

Why couldn't Mother Goose eat her soup?
Because the dish ran away with the spoon.

Why did Little Miss Muffet need directions?
She had lost her whey.

heavenly sciences

What is an astronaut's favorite meal?
Launch!

Why did the astronaut keep changing his course?
He didn't take the time to plan-et!

What's it called when a spaceman does karate?
Martian arts.

How do you know that the sun is lighter than the earth?
It rises in the sky every morning.

What is the moon worth?
  Four quarters.

How does the sun take a nap?
  It sets for awhile.

What goes up when you count down?
  A rocket.

Why do people like jokes about rockets?
  Because they're a blast.

Why is the law of gravity untrustworthy?
  It will always let you down.

What do meteorologists call the end of a dry spell?
  A rainy day.

How do the stars keep squeaky clean?
  They use meteor showers.

If athletes get athletes foot, what do astronauts get?

Missle-toe (Mistletoe).

Why did Mr. Twice tell his children to play outside during the thunderstorm?

Because everyone knows that lightning doesn't strike twice.

What is light enough to caress the sky, gentle enough to soothe the skin, and hard enough to crack rocks?

Water.

What illness did everyone on *Star Trek* catch?

Chicken Spocks!

What kind of flowers do you find on the sun?

Sunflowers.

What type of beam is the lightest?

A moonbeam.

What can fall but will never break, and what can break but will never fall?
Night and day.

Why did the thermometer go to college?
He wanted to get his degree.

Where do stars and planets go to school?
At the universe-ity.

What can travel around the world without ever needing gas?
The moon.

Why will the sun always get the highest grades in school?
Because he is so bright.

What existed since the world began but is never more than one month old?
The moon.

At what time is it hard to land on the moon?
  When it is full.

Why did the sheriff arrest the stars?
  They were caught shooting.

history and geography

Why is Alabama the smartest state in the United States?
Because it has four A's and one B!

How did the colonists react to the sugar tax?
They raised cane.

What is the best state to buy a small bottle of cola?
Mini Soda (Minnesota).

What is the most slippery country in the world?
Greece.

Why did George Washington sleep sitting up?
Because he couldn't lie.

What bus sailed across the Atlantic Ocean?
Columbus.

How did Betsy Ross judge her work?
"Sew, sew."

What state of the United States plays church music?
Oregon.

What country gets all stirred up?
Mix-i-co (Mexico).

How was the Roman Empire cut in half?
With a pair of Caesars!

What state is always sick?
Ill-inois.

What did Delaware do when Mississippi lent Missouri her New Jersey?

I don't know, Alaska.

What did Napoleon become after his thirty-ninth birthday?

Forty years old.

Why did Benjamin Franklin like flying his kite?

He always got a charge out of it.

How did the Vikings send secret messages?

By Norse code.

Where was the Declaration of Independence signed?

At the bottom.

Which state is surrounded by the most water?

Hawaii. All of it is surrounded by water.

How much did the pirate pay for his earrings?
A buccaneer.

Which U.S. President liked to clean house?
Hoover.

What kind of knights rode camels?
The Arabian knights.

Who invented King Arthur's round table?
Sir Cumference.

Where did the Pilgrims land when they reached America?
On their feet.

What state can you walk all over?
Floor-ida.

What newspaper did the dinosaurs prefer?
The Prehistoric Times.

What famous philosopher was known for his many carriages?
Des-cart-es.

What are prehistoric monsters called when they sleep?
A dinosnore.

How did Columbus's men sleep on their ships?
With their eyes shut!

What is the fruitiest of all school subjects?
History, because it's full of dates!

Why were the early days of history called the dark ages?
Because there were so many knights!

If April showers bring May flowers, what do May flowers bring?
Pilgrims.

Why does the Statue of Liberty stand in New York harbor?
Because she can't sit down!

What did Paul Revere say at the end of his famous ride?
Whoa!

What did King George say when he heard about the rebellious American colonies?
"How revolting!"

What goes from Maine to Florida without moving?
The highway.

What state is the cleanest?
Wash-ington.

What did the world call Thomas Edison's invention of the light bulb?
A bright idea.

What was Camelot?
A place where people parked their camels.

Where was Solomon's temple?
Near his cheek.

What would you call theft in Peking?
A Chinese takeout!

Where did Paul Bunyan file his axe?
Under the letter A.

Where is the biggest pencil in the world?
Pencil-vania.

How can you name the capital of every U.S. state in two seconds?
Say, "Washington, DC."

What country makes you shiver?
Chile.

What state is the smallest?
  Minnisota (mini-sota).

What are the only two states that have their state name in their state capital?
  Oklahoma and Indiana.

Why were the Indians the first people in North America?
  They had reservations.

What rock group has four members, all of whom are dead, one of which was assassinated?
  Mt. Rushmore.

Where did Abraham Lincoln sign the Emancipation Proclamation?
  At the bottom of the last page.

What were the first words out of Alexander Graham Bell's mouth?
  "Mama" and "Dada."

Where do you find Timbuktu?
Between Timbuk-one and Timbuk-three.

What did Mason say to Dixon?
"We have to draw the line."

What was the colonist's favorite drink?
Liber-Tea.

What has four eyes but can't see?
Mississippi.

What do you call people who are always in a hurry?
Russians.

What country constantly has rain?
Bah-rain.

What did the flag say to Thomas Jefferson?
Nothing. It just waved.

What do you call people who like to travel a lot?
Romans.

What do history teachers talk about when they get together?
The old days.

How were Martha Washington's wigs delivered?
By hair mail.

When is a piece of wood like Queen Elizabeth?
When the piece of wood is a ruler.

How is the United States similar to a marathon runner?
They both have healthy constitutions.

What is the rope that you never jump with?
Europe.

Which vegetable wasn't allowed on
Columbus's ships?
The leek.

What would happen if you threw a white
rock into the Black Sea?
It would get wet.

Where can you find roads without cars, forests
without trees, and cities without houses?
On a map.

If King Henry VIII were alive today, what
would he be most famous for?
Extreme old age.

What is found in the middle of America and
Australia?
The letter R.

Before scientists traveled down the Nile River,
what was the longest river in the world?
The Nile River.

What part of the Great Wall of China did the Chinese not design?
The cracks.

how do you. . . ?

How do you stop a bull from charging?
Take away its credit card.

How do you keep a skunk from smelling?
Hold its nose.

How do you move a dinosaur's toe?
With a toe-truck.

How do you put out a fire at the post office?
Stamp it out.

How do you make an eggroll?
You push it.

How do you know if there is any bread in the house?

Have a roll call.

How do you say Peter picked a peck of pickled peppers in Russian?

Peter picked a peck of pickled peppers in Russian.

How do you get into a haunted house?

With a skeleton key.

How do you strike it rich in sports?

Become a professional bowler.

How do you make "one" vanish?

Add a "g" for "gone" or an "n" to change it to "none"!

How do you know when a mathematician is dead?

His number is up.

How do you make a hot dog stand?
   Steal its chair.

How do you carry Abraham Lincoln in your left and right hand pockets?
   You put a penny with Lincoln's image in your left hand pocket and a five dollar bill with Lincoln's picture in your right hand pocket.

How do you catch a unique rabbit?
   Unique up on it!

How do you catch a tame rabbit?
   Tame way. Unique up on it!

How do you make an odd number even?
   Take away the s in seven and you have even.

How do you clear ice off of tall buildings?
   Use sky scrapers.

How do you keep a rhino from charging?
Take away its credit card!

How do you avoid being driven crazy?
Walk.

How do you get a road to talk?
Use "sign" language.

How do you make an elephant stew?
You keep it waiting for a few hours.

How do you know when there is a squirrel
in the peanut butter?
Check the ingredients.

How do you make a lemon drop?
You hold it in the air and then let it go.

How do you make a fire with two sticks?
Make sure one of the sticks is a match.

How do you name three consecutive days without using the words Monday, Tuesday, Wednesday, Thursday, Friday, Saturday, or Sunday?

Yesterday, Today, and Tomorrow!

How do you find the most successful salesman?

Look on the best-seller list.

How do you tell if the chimney is sick?

Check for the flu.

How do you know if your sewing machine is sick?

It just won't seam right.

How do you make anti-freeze?

Put ice in her bed.

How do you add two to eleven and get one?

Add two hours to eleven o'clock and you will get one o'clock.

How do you get across the Nottafoot River
without using a canoe?
*You walk. The Nottafoot River is only
eleven inches deep.*

human nature

Where do you find a roof that is always wet?
The roof of your mouth.

What belongs to you, but other people use it more often?
Your name.

What part of your body is helpful during the Boston Marathon?
A runny nose.

What does your friend have to take before you can receive it?
Your photo.

What is the easiest thing to part with?
A comb.

Who can marry many women but still
remain single?
A minister.

How many men were born in 1920?
None. Only babies were born.

What cap is never removed?
Your knee cap.

How do you tell a lazy man by his shoes?
See if he is wearing loafers.

What is the favorite color of the human nose?
Blew.

What do you do to get your eyes dressed up?
You clothes them.

What question can you never answer with a "yes"?

"Are you sleeping?"

What boy likes to hang out by the front door?

Matt.

What is the one thing you can always count on?

Your fingers.

What part of the body is the most popular?

The tonsils because they are always being scheduled to come out.

What did the rib cage say to the heart and lungs?

"Got you covered!"

What joins two people but only touches one?

A wedding ring.

When does your nose smell the worst?
When it is stuffed up.

What do Christians take when they have a cold?
Gos-pills.

What happened to Samuel Taylor when he married an aunt?
He became Uncle Sam.

How tall are you when you do a handstand?
Two feet high.

What is over your head and under your hat?
Your hair.

What part of your body has the most rhythm?
Your eardrums.

What can you hold without ever touching it?
A conversation.

In which month do people exercise the least?
February—it's the shortest month.

What are the most lucrative teeth to leave for the tooth fairy?
Buck teeth.

The person sitting in the living room is not your sibling but she is a child of your mother and father. Who is that person?
You.

When does your lap disappear?
When you stand up.

How did the man feel when he received his electric bill?
He was shocked!

What part of the human body is most like a tree?
The palms.

Why was the fireman lonely and sad?
He missed his old flame.

What do Eskimos get from sitting on the ice too long?
Polaroids.

Why are talkative people generally overweight?
They like to chew the fat.

What office job do fingernails dislike the most?
Filing.

How do chess players tell fairy tales?
"Once a-pawn a time. . ."

What can you say about a girl named Sugar?
She is probably refined.

Where do twins usually sleep?
In double beds.

What boy is always around to fix your flat tire?
  Jack.

What kind of animals do most people own?
  Calves.

What do you leave behind only after you take?
  Footstep.

What is the one thing that every human being has had except for Adam and Eve?
  Parents.

What walks on four legs in the morning, two legs in the afternoon, and three legs in the evening? (Riddle of the Sphinx)
  A man—crawls as a baby, walks as an adult, and uses a cane when elderly.

Why did the wandering traveler burn down her house?
  She loved home cooking.

What counts up but never counts down?
Your age.

What did Sarah try to use to replace her lost tooth?
Toothpaste.

What is the best way to avoid hitting your fingers with a hammer?
Hold the hammer with both hands.

What do you call a girl who always has change?
Penny.

Can you name something that you get to keep even when you give it to someone?
Your word.

What do you call an Aunt who runs off to get married?
An Antelope.

What is the best way to eliminate wrinkles?
With an iron.

What should you do if your ears are ringing?
Answer them.

What do people make that you can't see?
Noise.

Why did the two hairs say farewell?
They knew parting was such sweet sorrow.

What is a good name for lawyers?
Sue.

What is a good name for a thief?
Rob.

If Bob's father is Ben's son, what relation is Bob to Ben?
Ben is Bob's grandfather.

How can Sarah physically stand behind Kate
if Kate is physically standing behind Sarah?
The two girls are standing back to back.

What gets darker as the room becomes
lighter?
Your shadow.

What do opticians call their annual dance?
The eye ball.

Why did the aging climber quit hiking?
He was already over the hill.

What can you catch but not hold?
A cold.

What is the oldest part of a man's body?
*The Adam's apple. It has been there since
the beginning.*

in the kitchen

What is the best way to keep food bills down?
With a paperweight!

How can you tell the difference between a can of chicken soup and a can of turkey soup?
Read the label.

What did the mayonnaise say to the refrigerator?
"Close the door! I'm dressing."

What kind of soda is dangerous to drink?
Baking soda.

What kind of food will you find in heaven?
Angel food cake.

Why was the ketchup last in the race?
It couldn't catch up.

What vegetable will bring you good luck?
Garluck.

What has four legs, a head, and leaves?
A dining room table.

What did the hotdog say when he won the race?
I'm the wiener.

When do you find pickles at the door?
When it is ajar.

What did the chef say to the Caesar salad?
You are big enough to get dressed yourself.

What's green and bores holes?
A drill pickle.

What do you call an apple with a short temper?
A crab apple.

What food can you catch a virus from?
Wheat germ.

Why did the cabbage win the race?
It was a-HEAD!

What kind of nut comes without a shell?
A doughnut.

What did the banana say to the orange?
I'm PEELING so loved!

What is most useful when it has been broken?
An egg.

Why did Ms. Melon refuse the marriage proposal?
  "Because I cantaloupe!"

How do you know if a chef is in trouble?
  See if his goose is cooked.

What rises every morning but is not the sun?
  The bread in a bakery.

What did the refrigerator say to the milk?
  "Don't come in! I've got a cold!"

Where do hot dogs dance?
  At meatballs.

When was meat the highest it has ever been?
  When the cow jumped over the moon.

What book has the most stirring topics?
  A cookbook.

What is black when you buy it, red when you use it, and gray when you throw it away?
Charcoal.

Why shouldn't you tell secrets around produce?
The corn has ears, the potatoes have eyes, and the beanstalk.

What can be peeled and chipped, but will never crack?
A potato.

What dessert comes in an edible container?
An ice cream cone.

What soup is good for your brain?
Noodle soup.

Where did the cup and saucer go for vacations?
To China.

Why did the hot dog wear a sweater?
Because it was a chili dog.

What is always better before it is cooked?
Anything burnt.

How do you get water into a watermelon?
You plant it in the spring.

How did Sally flatter the potato?
She buttered it up.

Why did the sub sandwich get a medal?
Because he was a hero.

What is the smallest room in the world?
A mushroom.

What did the vegetables say after getting stuck in the fridge?
"Lettuce out!"

Which of these fruits does not belong: apple, peach, banana, strawberry, pear?

The banana. It's the only one that needs to be peeled before eating.

What kind of drink will give you a black and blue face?

Punch.

What lives in the ground and has eyes, but doesn't have a mouth or nose?

A potato.

Name two things you can't have for breakfast.

Lunch and dinner.

What kind of apple isn't an apple?

A pineapple.

Why is the cookie so bitter?

It has a chip on its shoulder.

What did the zombie always put on his
mashed potatoes?
    Grave-y.

What fruits are most often mentioned in
history?
    Dates.

Why was the chef arrested?
    *He was caught beating the eggs and whip-
    ping the cream.*

What do you always find asleep in the dining room?
    Napkins.

What kind of coffee do you drink on the
train?
    Expresso.

What always stays hot even in the refrigerator?
    Salsa.

What has to be broken before it is eaten?
An egg.

What vegetable has the best rhythm?
Beets.

What kind of berry did B.B. King like to eat?
Blueberries.

What kind of cheese did Frankenstein like?
Muenster.

What vegetable has the best eyesight?
Potatoes because they have so many eyes.

What cereal always puts a smile on your face?
Grinola.

What looks just like half an apple?
The other half.

What fruit goes well with any drink?
Strawberries.

What kind of cup has trouble holding water?
A cupcake.

How do you know when the grapes are old and tired?
They start to wine.

What is the best way to make meatloaf?
Send your cow on vacation.

What fruit is often hired by the Navy?
Naval oranges.

Why won't you ever find a lonely banana?
Because they always stay in bunches.

How do salad dressings like to sleep?
On a bed of lettuce.

What kind of jam can't you eat?
A traffic jam.

Why wasn't the girl hurt when she fell into a puddle of Coke?
Because it was a soft drink.

jungle fever

What do lions wear to bed?
  Striped pajamas.

What did the leopards say when they ran
into one another?
  "Boy! That hit the spot!"

What would you do if an elephant sat in
front of you at the movies?
  Miss most of the movie.

How do you know if an elephant plans to
stay the weekend?
  See if he brought his trunk.

What was the elephant doing on Route 325?
About four miles per hour.

Why are elephants cheaper to employ than any other animal?
Elephants will work for peanuts.

How does an elephant climb a tree?
It sits on an acorn and waits.

What time is it when an elephant sits on your fence?
Time to get a new fence.

What happened when the lion ate the comedian?
He felt funny.

Why did the two elephants get sent from the pool?
They only had a pair of trunks between them.

What does a lion brush his mane with?

A catacomb.

What's the difference between a tiger and a lion?

A tiger has the mane part missing.

What happens when a lion runs into an express train at the station?

It's the end of the lion.

What does the lion say to his friends before they go out hunting for food?

"Let us prey."

What is the best thing to do if you find a gorilla in your fridge?

Find something else to eat.

What always follows a tiger when he goes on vacation?

His tail.

Why did the elephant go to the luggage shop?
To buy a new trunk.

What do you call a lion that has eaten your mother's sister?
An aunt-eater.

What big cat should you never play a card game with?
A cheetah.

What vegetable do you get when an elephant walks through your garden?
Squash.

What would you get if you crossed a blimp with an orangutan?
A hot-air baboon.

How many lions can you fit into an empty cage?
One. After that, it isn't empty anymore.

Why is it hard to spot a leopard in the jungle?
Because they are born spotted.

How do you fix a broken chimp?
With a monkey wrench.

literature

Who wrote "I Love School?"
I. M. Kidding.

Who wrote "America's Longest River?"
Missy Sippy.

Who wrote "French Overpopulation?"
Francis Crowded.

Who wrote "The Color of Eggs?"
Summer Brown.

Who wrote, "Lost in the Forest?"
Miss Sing.

Who wrote "Building the Really Tall Skyscraper"
Linda Hand.

Who wrote "I Can Fly?"
Ima Byrd.

Who wrote "No Fear of Dentists?"
Dr. I. Pullem.

Who wrote "The New Shoes?"
Ben Down and Tye Laces.

Who wrote "The Haunted Mansion?"
Hugo First.

Who wrote "The World's Softest Toys?"
Ted E. Bear.

Who wrote "How I Really Feel?"
Olive Ewe.

Who wrote "How to Stay Home from
School?"
    Fay King.

Who wrote "How to Cook Wild Game?"
    Chris P. Duck.

Who wrote "The Long Walk Home?"
    Miss D. Buss

Who wrote "The Greatest and the Least?"
    Maxi Mum and Mini Mum

Who likes to make dinner for Moby Dick?
    Captain Cook.

Where did Sherlock Holmes go to school?
    Elementary, Dear Watson.

What is Dr. Jekyll's favorite game?
    Hyde and seek.

Who wrote "Dinosaurs and Other Primitive Tales?"

T. Rex.

What does Winnie the Pooh plan to do after his wedding?

Go on the honey-moon.

How does a book insult a newspaper?

By calling it spineless.

What was Agatha Christie's pen name?

She didn't have a name for her pen.

make like a tree and leave

What tree is always unhappy?
The blue spruce.

Where do walnuts look for their brothers and sisters?
In the family tree.

Why did the man cut down the tree that suddenly grew up in his yard?
Because it was tree-passing.

What's the best way to catch a squirrel?
Climb a tree and act like a nut.

What has four legs, and is green and fuzzy?
A pool table!

How do trees like to eat ice cream?
In pinecones.

Which tree is dressed the warmest?
A fir tree.

What does a tree do when he is ready to go home?
He leaves.

Which tree spends the most time on vacation?
A beech tree.

Why is a tree surgeon like an actor?
Because he's always taking boughs.

Why was the leaf sent to the hospital?
He had a bad fall.

What did the tree say to the other tree?
Leaf me alone.

Why was the dog mad at the tree?
Because the tree had its bark.

What goes around the tree but never goes into the tree?
The bark.

What is the tree's favorite drink?
Root beer.

Which tree has the loudest bark?
The dogwood.

Where did the gardener go for training?
Nursery school.

What did the tree say to the woodpecker?
"Leaf me alone."

Where do you go to find information about trees?
   The branch library.

What did the tree say to his friend at the end of the day?
   "I have to leaf."

What kind of tree is only found in a house?
   A pantry.

Why was the lumberjack afraid of trees?
   He thought their bite was worse than their bark.

What did the tree shout at the football match?
   I am rooting for you!

Where do the baby trees go to school?
   At a nursery.

One day, a young boy climbed a tall maple tree in order to gather acorns. After two hours, he still had not found any acorns. Why not?

Acorns don't grow on maple trees. They grow on oak trees.

odds and ends

How many three cent stamps are in a dozen?
There are twelve three cent stamps in a dozen.

When does saying something's name kill it?
Silence.

What is purchased by the yard and used by the foot?
Carpet.

What is big when it is new but gets smaller with each use?
A bar of soap.

What goes up and down but doesn't move?
A staircase.

What is the saddest time of the day?
Mourning.

What would you get if seven hundred stamps
were running one hundred miles per hour?
A stampede.

What consumes itself and dies as soon as it
is devoured?
A candle.

What three things have eyes but cannot see?
Needles, potatoes, and hurricanes.

What kind of clothing do cities wear?
Outskirts.

What can run but can't walk?
Water.

What can go up a chimney down, but will never go down a chimney up?
An umbrella.

What has no substance yet you can still see it?
A hole!

What goes around the yard but never moves?
A fence.

What did the cold computer say to the camp fire?
"Log on."

What has wheels and flies?
A garbage truck.

What has four legs but only one foot?
A bed.

Where did the city store its taxis?
In a cab-inet.

Why did the hikers find Mt. Washington so funny?

It was hill-arious.

What points up when it's light but points down when it is dark?

A light switch.

Which is heavier, a pound of feathers or a pound of bricks?

Neither. Both groups weigh exactly one pound.

What color is always screaming?

Yell-ow!

What musical instrument has the best character?

The upright piano.

What makes a chess player happy?

Taking the knight off.

What has a head and a tail, is brown, but has no legs?

A penny.

What can you draw without a pencil or paper?

A window shade.

What musical instrument do computers like to play?

The keyboard.

What goes up when the rain begins to come down?

Your umbrella.

What did one elevator say to the other elevator?

"I am coming down with something."

What goes all over the world yet stays in a corner?

A stamp.

How many sides does a circle have?
Two. The inside and the outside.

What can run but will not walk, has a mouth but will not talk, has a bed but will not sleep?
A river.

Why does B.B. King keep his guitar in the fridge?
He likes cool music.

What did one wall say to the other?
"Meet me in the corner."

What is the first sign that your computer is getting old?
Memory loss.

What would be worse than finding a worm in your apple?
Finding half a worm in your apple!

What did the rug say to the floor?
"Don't move; I've got you covered."

Which two words contain the most letters?
Post office.

What did one magnet say to the other?
"I find you very attractive."

When does a chair dislike you?
When it can't bear you.

What is the best day to go to the beach?
Sun-day.

What can fly when it is on and float when it is off?
A feather.

Why was the computer declared a hero?
He was always saving things.

What did the necktie say to the hat?
  "You go on ahead. I'll hang around for a while."

How did the fireplace feel?
  Grate!

Who can jump higher than a house?
  Anyone. A house can't jump.

What building has the most stories?
  A library!

How did the rain make the ghost upset?
  It dampened her spirits.

What piece of wood is like a king?
  A ruler.

What did the window say to the nurse?
  "I have this pane."

What office supply company is always going out of business?
Disappearing Inc.

What is easy to return but impossible to borrow?
Gratitude.

What has fifty heads and fifty tails?
A roll of pennies.

What asks no question but demands an answer?
The doorbell.

In what language do baked goods communicate?
Danish.

What has a fork and mouth, but never eats food?
A river.

What doesn't have wings, but can fly?
A cloud.

What grows bigger the more you take from it?
A hole in the ground.

What kind of soap do telephones use?
Dial.

Did you hear about the two telephones that got married?
It was a double ring ceremony.

What is another name for a telephone booth?
A chatterbox.

What is the smallest boat in the world?
A fairy (ferry) boat!

What never was, but always will be?
Tomorrow.

What is the best thing to take into the desert?

A thirst aid kit.

What has three legs when resting but only one leg when working?

A wheelbarrow.

Where do you find good sandwiches in India?

Try New Delhi.

Why wouldn't Silly Sam walk barefoot in the grass?

Because it was full of blades.

Which months of the year have twenty-eight days?

All of them.

What time is it when a clock strikes thirteen?

Time to get a new clock.

What kind of lights did Noah have on the ark?

Floodlights.

What can travel all the way around the world and still stay in one corner?

A postage stamp.

What has an eye but cannot see?

A needle.

What did the clock's big hand say to the little hand?

"I'll see you in an hour."

What moves around all day and sits in your room at night with its tongue hanging out?

A shoe.

What never gets sick but is always broken out with twenty-one spots?

A six sided die.

What kind of paper makes you itch?
Scratch paper.

Do you say "Eight and Four is Eleven" or
"Eight and Four are Eleven"?
Neither. Eight and Four is Twelve.

What is strong enough to hold a stone but
can't hold water?
A sieve.

How did Igor know where to find
Frankenstein?
He had a hunch.

What are the strongest days of the week?
*Saturday and Sunday. All other days are
weak (week) days!*

What is the only thing left after a train goes
by?
Its tracks.

Who was the best actor in the Bible?
Samson. He brought the house down!

What is the favorite mode of transportation
for accountants?
Tax-is.

What mode of transportation travels faster
than most cars yet can also pass through a
mountain?
A train.

Where should you go to buy a bed spread?
Downtown.

What did the mother book say to her son
before he left for the playground?
"Don't lose your jacket!"

What day of the week is named after a
number?
Two's day.

What holds water but is full of holes?
  A sponge.

What do you call the science of shopping?
  Buy-ology.

Where is the Goodyear Blimp stored?
  In a high rise facility.

What is the best way to catch a bus?
  On a corner.

What season do skydivers love the best?
  Fall.

What can you feed and it will grow, but give it water and it will die?
  Fire.

Where did Billy the Kid have his art show?
  At the shooting gallery.

What does Payless Shoes call its annual holiday party?
The foot ball.

What has nothing left but a nose after you remove its eye?
Noise.

When is a door not a door?
When it's ajar.

When is a house not a house?
When it's afire.

puppies and kittens

What bone will a dog never eat?
   A trombone.

When does a man act like a dog?
   When he's a boxer.

What do you get when you put a kitten in a Xerox machine?
   A copycat.

If ten cats were on a boat and one jumped off, how many were left?
   None, they were all copycats!

How does a dog turn off the VCR?
He presses the PAWS button.

What do cats like to read?
Mews-papers.

What is noisier than a cat stuck in a tree?
Two cats stuck in a tree.

Why was the cat afraid of the tree?
Because the cat heard it barked.

Where do you find a dog with no legs?
Right where you left him.

What did the dog say to the tree?
"Bark! Bark!"

What do you have to know to teach your dog tricks?
More than your dog.

What do you call a lemon eating cat?
A sourpuss.

What do you call a puppy in January?
A chili dog.

What do you get when you cross Lassie with a petunia?
A Collie flower.

What do cats call rodents on skateboards?
Meals on wheels.

What kind of dog works for scientists?
A lab.

What do you call a dog with a cold?
Germy shepherd.

What do you call a poodle in a sauna?
A hot dog.

Where do little dogs sleep when they go camping?

In pup tents.

What do you get if you cross a pointer with a Christmas tree?

A poinsettia.

How do you spell "mousetrap" using three letters?

C-A-T.

What dog can jump higher than a tree?

Any dog can jump higher than a tree. Trees don't jump.

What kind of carry-on did the puppy take on his trip?

A doggie bag.

What animal keeps the best time?

A watch dog.

What did the Australian delegate from the
U.N. name his dog?
Diplo-mutt.

What kind of dog watches NASCAR racing?
A lap dog.

When will a white dog enter a blue house?
Only when the door is open.

How did the dogs get rid of pounds?
They went on a diet.

What do you say when Fido eats your clock?
Alarming!

Why do cats make the best pets?
They are purr-fect.

Why did the dog sit in the shade?
He didn't want to be a hot dog.

What happened when Tommy's dog ate his watch?

The dog got lots of ticks.

school days

What school subject are snakes best at?
Hiss-tory.

Where does Winnie the Pooh keep his lunch box at school?
In his cubby.

How did a boy that was failing every subject get to high school?
He rode the bus.

What kind of cruise do college students travel on?
A scholar-ship.

What tools do you need in math class?
Multi-pliers.

Why did the teacher yell at the student for
something she didn't do?
She didn't do her homework.

Why did the teacher put the lights on?
Because the class was so dim!

What do English teachers eat for lunch?
Alphabet soup.

What is a forum?
Two-um plus two-um!

Where did the swim team meet for lunch?
At the pool table.

Why did the boy take a ladder to school?
Because he now goes to high school!

What did the Second Grade math book say to the First Grade math book?
I have a lot of problems.

What would you get if you crossed a vampire and a teacher?
Lots of blood tests!

Where do you go to school to learn how to greet people?
Hi school.

Which which teacher teacher always always uses uses words words twice twice?
A history teacher because history always repeats itself.

What do elves do after school?
Gnomework.

How do you pass a geometry test?
Memorize all the angles.

Why did the boy go to night school?
Because he wanted to learn how to read in the dark.

If you have fifty dollars in one coat pocket and fifty dollars in the other pocket, what do you have?
Most likely, the wrong coat!

Why did the math teacher cry on the last day of school?
He hates being divided from his class.

Why couldn't the skeleton go to school?
He didn't have the brain for it.

What is the worst thing you'll find in a school cafeteria?
The food.

What kind of table is in every school?
A multiplication table!

When does a student start dreaming of summer vacation?
When he is asleep.

How did the silly choir director tell her students to reach the high notes?
Stand on a chair.

What is the hardest subject in school?
The study of rocks.

How do school supplies escape from their desks?
They use the compass to find their way out.

What does a school teacher have in common with an eye doctor?
They both stare at pupils.

What happened to the principal who fell into the copying machine?
She was beside herself!

What is yellow and arrives at the door to make a mother's load lighter?
The school bus.

What is another name for a bunch of bees?
A good report card.

What kind of students are postal workers?
First class.

How does a bee get to school?
It takes the buzz.

Which grade is never tardy?
"Second" grade.

What is the favorite drink of cheerleaders?
Root beer.

What did the calculator say to the student?
You can count on me.

What did the first arithmetic book say to the other arithmetic book?

I really have a lot of problems!

What kind of skates do math students prefer?

Figure skates.

Why did Ms. Smith tell her students to use a table with no legs?

It was a multiplication table.

How many times can you subtract four from sixteen?

Once. Then you are subtracting from twelve.

Why did the boy eat his homework?

His teacher said it was a piece of cake.

spelling

What question must you always answer with a "yes?"
What does Y-E-S spell?

What always ends everything?
The letter G.

What can you find in the middle of nowhere?
The letter H!

How do you spell mousetrap using three letters?
C-A-T!

What ten-letter word starts with g-a-s?
  A-u-t-o-m-o-b-i-l-e.

Why is the letter A like a flower?
  Because the bee (B) comes after it.

When does Friday come before Thursday?
  In the dictionary!

What is at the center of gravity?
  The letter V!

What letter is always missing from the alphabet?
  The one you mail.

What three letters turn a boy into a man?
  A-G-E.

What's in the middle of the world?
  The letter R!

What eleven-letter English word does everyone pronounce incorrectly?
Incorrectly.

There is a word of three letters that will be fewer if you add two. What is it?
Few.

What word if pronounced right is wrong, but pronounced wrong is right?
Wrong.

What four letters are meant to bring the world to a stand still?
S-T-O-P.

If she sells sea shells by the sea shore, how many S's are in that?
None! (There are no S's in THAT)

Where do you always find happiness?
In the dictionary.

What makes a road broad?
The letter R.

What common English word can be written backward, forward, or upside down without changing?
NOON.

What starts with 'T' ends with 'T' and is full with 'T'?
A teapot.

How many words can you make from "new door"?
One word. (Literally, o-n-e w-o-r-d)

What is never out of fashion but always out of date?
The letter F.

Why did Lucy like the letter K?
It makes Lucy lucky.

What letter comes after B in the alphabet?
The letter E.

How many letters are in the alphabet?
There are eleven letters in "the alphabet."

What tastes hot, but has ice in it?
SPICE.

What do you find the alphabet doing at the end of the day?
Catching a few more ZZZZZs.

Have you ever seen a duchess?
Yes—it's the same as an English "s"!

What is in the middle of the sun?
The letter U.

What letter is nine inches long?
The letter Y. It is one-quarter of a yard.

How can the word *candy* be spelled with only two letters?
   C and Y.

Can you spell cold water with three letters?
   I-C-E.

What letter in the alphabet has a problem with envy?
   Jealous E.

take me out
to the ballgame

What do baseball games and pancakes have in common?

It's all about the batter.

How do you figure a basketball player's salary?

Find out his net worth.

What is the best way to learn golfing?

Take a course.

Why won't baseball players form a union?

They like to avoid strikes.

Why is a catcher's mitt like the chicken pox?
Both are catching.

Why wouldn't the cowardly baseball player
run to home base?
He was afraid of masked men.

What sport do shoes like to play?
Socker.

Where did the baseball player keep his mitt?
In the glove compartment.

What are basketball players' favorite stories?
Tall tales.

Why was the pig kicked off the soccer team?
He hogged the ball.

What do hungry golfers eat for lunch?
Their sand wedges.

What dish do football players like to use for breakfast?

The super bowl.

Wayne bets Tom twenty-five dollars that he can predict the score of the football game before it starts. Tom agrees, but loses the bet. Why did Tom lose the bet?

Wayne said the score would be 0–0 and he was right. "Before" any football game starts, the score is always 0–0.

What is a cheerleaders favorite drink?

Root beer.

What do cheerleaders like to eat for breakfast?

Cheer-ios.

What has two wings but can't fly?

A hockey team.

What is served but never eaten?

A tennis ball.

How does the captain of the football team get to games?
He flies coach.

What is the best way to stay cool at a ballgame?
Sit next to a fan.

Why do basketball players eat donuts when they snack?
They like to dunk.

What do tennis players and waitresses have in common?
They both like to serve.

What is another name for a fumble in football?
A field trip.

What football player wears the biggest pads?
The one with the biggest body.

Why are baseball players like prize-winning novelists?

Both of them are interested in runaway hits.

How do you stay in contact with a baseball player?

You touch base every so often.

Which baseball player is in charge of refreshments?

The pitcher.

Why were the tennis players kicked out of their apartment building?

They made too much of a racket (racquet).

Why do baseball players wear really old socks?

They like to have runs in their shoes.

What is the best diet for a golfer?

Greens only.

Why can't a baseball player be afraid of the dark?

He will always have to start with the miners.

What sport comes after nine but before eleven?

Ten-nis.

What can be driven without any wheels and can be sliced without a knife?

A golf ball.

What is the biggest diamond in the world?

A baseball diamond.

When should you get advice from football players and prisoners?

When you are weighing the pros and cons.

Why is an umpire like a telemarketer?

He is always making calls.

How did the farm team win the baseball game?

Their last little piggy ran all the way home.

What do you call a football player who never graduated from high school?

A left back.

Where do basketball players go to press charges?

The court.

What state supplies all sports uniforms?

New Jersey.

What sport are dishes particularly good at?

Bowl-ing.

What word makes baseball players angry but bowlers happy?

"Strike!"

Why is baseball such a cool game?
Because of all the fans.

What sport requires a carpet?
Rug-by.

When is baseball first mentioned in the Bible?
Genesis 1:1—"In the beginning (big inning). . ."

Who was the first tennis player in the Bible?
Joseph—he served in Pharaoh's court.

the buzz word

What did the flower say to the bee?
Buzz off!

Why won't you ever find a fat glowworm?
Because they only eat light meals!

What did the other flower say to the bee?
Quit bugging me!

What do bees wear in the swimming pool?
BEE-kinis.

What insect can be spelled with one letter?
B(ee).

Why didn't the fly go near the computer?
Because he was afraid he would get caught in the Web!

What did the bee teacher say to the naughty bee?
Bee-hive yourself!

What do you call two insects that have children?
Pair-ants.

What kind of bee is always dropping the football?
A fumblebee.

What do you get if you cross a bee with a doorbell?
A hum dinger.

What do bees do with their honey?
They cell it.

What is the insect's favorite game?
Cricket.

Why didn't the fly go near the computer?
Because he was afraid he would get caught in the Web.

What is green and can jump a mile in a minute?
A grasshopper with hiccups.

If there are seven flies in the kitchen, how can you tell which one is the cowboy?
Look for the one that is on the Range.

Why didn't the bee get an invitation to the dance?
It was a moth ball.

What did the bee say to his friend the flower?
"You are my best bud."

What do you call a bug's uncle's wife?
His ant.

What did the bee say to his barber?
"Just give me a buzz."

Why was the insect asked to leave the park?
He was a litterbug.

What do you call a nervous insect?
Jitterbug.

What did the bee tenant say to his visitor?
"I'll buzz you in."

What do you call a new bee?
A babe-bee.

What kind of bee has a hard time making up its mind?
A may-bee.

What insect is built by a blacksmith?
He makes the firefly.

Why do spiders make the best baseball players?
They are known for catching flies.

What did Mr. Bee say when he arrived home?
"Hi, Honey."

What kind of bee wins awards at school?
A spelling bee.

under the sea

What is the best way to catch a school of fish?
Use a bookworm.

What kind of fish should you use to make a peanut butter sandwich?
Jelly fish.

What kind of candy do blowfish love?
Bubble gum.

What doesn't get any wetter no matter how hard it rains?
The ocean.

What kind of boat deteriorates in water?
An ice cream float.

What is wrong with polluting the ocean?
You make the sea sick.

What kind of sea creatures play poker?
Card sharks.

Why won't clams lend you money?
Because they are shellfish.

How does an octopus go into battle?
Fully armed.

What builds up castles, tears down mountains,
helps some to see, but makes others blind?
Sand.

What does an octopus wear when it is cold?
A coat of arms.

Why was the sailor afraid of geometry?
He heard the Bermuda Triangle will make you disappear.

Where is the ocean the deepest?
On the bottom.

What part of a fish weighs the most?
Its scales.

What kind of money do crabs use?
Sand dollars.

Lovely and round,
I shine with pale light,
Grown in the darkness,
A lady's delight.
What am I?
A pearl.

What shellfish likes to lift weights?
Mussels.

What is round as a dishpan, deep as a tub,
and still the oceans couldn't fill it up?
A sieve.

How did the boat show affection?
It hugged the shore.

Who is the seaweed dating?
He goes out with the tide.

What ship has two mates but no captain?
A courtship.

What is the most expensive fish?
Goldfish.

Why did the beach keep losing sand?
He was a shore loser.

Where is the best place for fish to sleep?
In a riverbed.

What kind of fruit do young sea creatures leave on their teachers' desks?

Crab apples.

What carries a weight in its belly, trees on its back, nails in its ribs, but has no feet?

A ship.

What fisherman's employment and Spanish instrument's name are the same?

Castanet.

What would you get if you crossed the Indian Ocean with chili powder?

Heat waves.

How does the Navy get supplies to the sailors?

It ships them.

What lies at the bottom of the ocean and twitches?

A nervous wreck!

Why do submarine captains have the best dental hygiene?
They use their Scope several times a day.

What do you call a furious watercraft?
A steamed ship.

What do sharks like to eat for lunch?
Peanut butter and jellyfish.

What animal is the best at fencing?
The swordfish.

Why are fish so smart?
Because they live in schools.

What do fish use to cover their floors?
Carp-et.

Why are fish afraid to play volleyball?
They might get caught in the net.

What do you throw out when you need it, but take in when you are done with it?
   An anchor.

What was the educated oyster's favorite category in Jeopardy?
   Pearls of wisdom.

What is lighter than the material it is made of and keeps most of itself hidden from sight?
   An iceberg.

What game do fish like playing the most?
   "Name That Tuna."

What is faster than a fish?
   Anything that can catch it.

Which of these does not belong—shark, dolphin, catfish?
   A dolphin because it is a mammal.

What is the ocean's favorite kitchen appliance?

The micro-wave.

Why do fish like to travel in schools?

They like the group rates.

What animal is a weight loss fanatic?

A fish. He carries his own scales around with him.

How can you tell a friendly ocean from a mean ocean?

The friendly ocean will always wave to you.

What part of a ship is made out of cards?

The deck.

what am I?

My color is white and I am used for cutting.
When I'm broken or stained, humans usually
pull me or fill me. I also function as a useful
tool for most animals.
What am I?
   Teeth.

I can sizzle like bacon, and I am made with
   an egg.
I have plenty of backbone, but lack a good
   leg.
I peel layers like an onion, but still remain
   whole.
I can be long, like a flagpole; yet fit in a hole.
What am I?
   A snake.

I am strongest when you view me whole, but
I am often found in other shapes. I move
the oceans with my incredible strength, and
an explorer with a name like 'powerful bicep'
was the first to walk on me.
What am I?

The Moon.

You can blow up my skin
And tie me up tight.
I can float through the air
Without a fear of heights.
What am I?

A balloon.

A wee man in a little red coat.
Staff in his hand, and stone in his throat.
What am I?

A cherry.

I am cracked; I am made.
I am told; I am played.
What am I?

A joke.

I have four legs, two sides, one foot, and one head.
Cozy and comfy when covered with a spread.
What am I?
A bed.

When full, I can point the way, but when empty, nothing moves me. I have two skins
—One outside and one inside.
What am I?
A glove.

I am the ruler of shovels.
I have a double.
I am as thin as a knife.
I have a wife.
What am I?
The King of Spades from a deck of cards.

I am as round as the moon, the color of fine silver, and the hole in my middle helps me to play.
What am I?
A compact disc.

The higher I climb, the hotter I become.
My crystal cage is always my home.
What am I?

Mercury in a thermometer.

I have three hands
That rotate regularly around and around;
My second hand is really last, and usually
makes a sound.
What am I?

A clock with a second hand.

Dark with white writing,
And smooth like a slate.
Teachers depend on me,
And students clean my face.
What am I?

A chalkboard or blackboard.

Thousands hord gold in this house, but
no human built it. Spears are busy keeping
watch, but no human guards it.
What is it?

A beehive.

They call me a man, but I'll never have a
    life.
I was given a body, but will never have a
    wife.
They made me a mouth, but I cannot sing.
Water gives me life and death comes in
    Spring.
What am I?
    A snowman.

What force and strength cannot break
    through,
I with barely a touch can do.
And many in the street would wait,
Were I not a friend to the gate.
What am I?
    A key.

I come in different shapes and sizes. Part of
me has curves; part of me is straight. You can
put me anywhere you like, but there is only
one right place for me.
What am I?
    A jigsaw puzzle.

My life is often a container of woe,
My leaves require assistance to turn just so.
Hard is my spine and my insides are pale,
Yet I'm always ready to tell a good tale.
What am I?
 A book.

I can speak every language ever known to
man, but I have never attended school and I
tend to bounce around.
What am I?
 An echo.

Bright as diamonds;
Loud as thunder;
Never still;
A thing of wonder.
What am I?
 Fireworks.

I am used to bat with, yet I never get a hit. I
am near a ball, yet it is never thrown.
What am I?
 Eyelashes.

Fire is often lit above me, and if you delete
my first letter, you will find where everyone
you have ever known was born.
What am I?
  The hearth.

I can be an excellent seamstress,
But my eye can't see a stitch that I sew.
What am I?
  A needle.

Though fluid at birth,
Don't shove me too far.
Beware if I break,
For the outcome may scar.
What am I?
  Glass.

Part carbon and part water,
But I am poison to fishes.
Many falsely claim my name,
I am the pause that refreshes.
What am I?
  A soda.

I am cold as steel, but made of flesh. Never
thirsty, but I surround myself with liquid.
What am I?

A fish.

I always tell the truth, and reflect everything
I see.
You'll find me in all shapes and sizes. What
could I be?

A mirror.

I cannot be felt, seen, or touched; yet I can
be found in everyone. My existence is always
in debate; yet I have my own style of music.
What am I?

A soul.

Once upon a time, there was a green house.
Inside the green house, there were white
    walls.
Inside the white walls there was red furniture.
Living in the house were lots of babies.
What is it?

A watermelon.

My life can be measured in hours, and I
serve by being devoured.
If thin, I am quick; If fat, I am slow.
I must always beware that wind is my foe.
What am I?

A candle.

You hope you never have it. But when you
do, you hope you never lose it.
What is it?

A lawsuit.

I am the briefest complete sentence in the
English language.
What am I?

*I am! (Complete sentences always require a
noun and verb. Imperative commands do
not count.)*

I never was, but will always be. As soon as I
arrive, then I am gone. Everyone depends on
me, but they don't always look forward to me.
What am I?

Tomorrow.

At night they come without being called
And move around without being walled.
But at the very first sign of light,
They disappear back into the night.
What are they?
   Stars.

Around three o'clock, I often bathe.
I like my water hot.
A part of me just seeps away,
And then I hit the spot.
What am I?
   A tea bag.

I am taken from a mine, and shut up in
a wooden case from which I am never
released. Yet, I am used by almost everyone.
What am I?
   Pencil lead.

Not an airplane, but I can float across the sky.
Not a river, but full of water am I.
What am I?
   A cloud.

Only one color, but many a size,
Stuck on the bottom, yet easily flies.
Present in sun, but never in rain,
Doing no harm, and feeling no pain.
What am I?
   Your shadow!

I can be pronounced as one letter, but I am
written with three.
Read from both ends, and I am steady as
a tree.
What am I?
   The word EYE.

I can be cool, but I am never cold.
I can be sorry, but I won't be guilty.
I can be spooked, but I can't be anxious.
I can be sweet, but I don't include candy.
I can be swallowed, but I will never be eaten.
What am I?
   Words with double letters.

I can be published,
I can be spoken,
I can be uncovered,
I can be broken.
What am I?
  News.

The beginning of eternity;
The end of time and space.
The beginning of every end,
And the end of every place.
What am I?
  The letter E.

With pointed teeth I sit and wait,
To join my victims and determine fate.
My bloodless subjects show no fright,
Even when I pounce for a single bite.
What am I?
  A stapler.

You can hear me calling, summoning with
   a bell;
You never know if I want to greet or sell.
What am I?

   A telephone.

I have many legs, but need assistance to
stand. I have a long neck, but no head or
eyes to see. I keep things clean, but I am
usually quite dirty.
What am I?

   A broom.

what do you call. . . ?

What do you call an Eskimo cow?
An Eskimoo.

What do you call a pig doing karate?
A pork chop.

What do you call four Spaniards in quicksand?
Quatro sinko

What do you call a ship worker who always wears a hat?
Cap-tain.

What do you call a fish with no eye?
  Fsh.

What do you call a bear without an ear?
  B.

What do you call a deer with no eyes?
  No eye-deer. (No idea)

What do you call a snail with no shell?
  Homeless.

What do you call a greasy chicken?
  A slick chick.

What do you call a bear who whines?
  WHINY the Pooh.

What do you call the finger that flips to the
end of a book?
  Your index finger.

What do you call a fly with no wings?
A walk.

What do you call a traveling flea?
An itch hiker.

What do you call an artistic bridge?
A drawbridge.

What do you call paper that will tear easily?
Terrible (tearable) paper.

What do you call a loud color?
Yellow.

What do you call two spiders that just got married?
Newlywebs.

What do you call a blind dinosaur?
Do-you-think-he-saurus.

What do you call a reptile with its own rap group?

A RAP-tile!

What do you call a dinosaur that sings?

A rockosaurus.

What do you call someone who snores?

A sound sleeper.

What do you call a sleeping dinosaur?

A bronto-SNORE-us.

What do you call a sleeping dinosaur?

A Sleepasaurus!

What do you call a dinosaur cowboy?

Tyrannosaurus Tex.

What do you call a doctor who treats his patients like animals?

A veterinarian.

What do you call a vehicle that has four wheels and flies?

A garbage truck.

What do you call the best time to jump on a trampoline?

Springtime.

What do you call a man with a shovel in his hand?

Doug.

What do you call a man WITHOUT a shovel in his hand?

Douglas.

What do you call a person who steals soap?

A dirty thief.

What do you call a man who hangs on a wall?

Art.

What do you call a girl who walks over
water?
   Bridget.

What do you call a man who works in
a garden?
   Bud.

What do you call a man who rakes leaves?
   Russell.

What do you call an unemployed court
jester?
   Nobody's fool.

What do you call a boomerang that doesn't
work?
   A stick.

What do you call the place where dishonest
people get their books?
   The lie-brary.

What do you call the best butter on the farm?
A goat.

What do you call a gathering of weird numbers?
Odd.

What do you call two backbones with a thousand ribs?
Railroad tracks.

What do you call something that everyone asks for, everyone gives, everyone needs, but very few people take?
Advice.

What do you call a country where everyone has to drive a red car?
A red carnation.

When is a cafeteria called a mess hall?
After a food fight.

What do you call a woman with big blue hair and funny wire glasses who takes a plane from Florida to California?
A passenger.

What do you call something that can fill a room but doesn't take up any space?
Light.

What do you call the music people listen to in the car?
Cartoons. (car-tunes)

What do you call a lazy doctor?
Dr. Doolittle.

What do you call a calf after it's six months old?
Seven months old.

What do you call cheese that isn't yours?
Nacho Cheese.

What do you call a writing instrument that doesn't have any hair?
A bald-point pen.

What do you call two banana peels?
A pair of slippers!

What do you call a dog at the beach?
A hot dog!

What do you call one piece of firewood?
A mono-log.

What do you call a rabbit with fleas?
Bugs Bunny.

What do you call a penguin in the desert?
Lost.

What do you call a watch worn on a belt?
A waist of time!

What do you call a man who shaves more than ten times a day?
A barber.

What do you call a window that can't pay its bills?
Broke.

What do you call a mushroom with a great sense of humor?
A fungi.

What do you call the man who repairs bicycles?
A spokesman.

What do you call a sleeping bull?
A bulldozer.

What do you call a bowling team made up of ministers?
The Holy Rollers.

What do you call a bird convict?
Robin Hood.

What do you call a mild mannered snake?
A civil serpent.

What do you call an object that is strong as good steel but is basically holes connected to more holes?
A chain.

What do you call a bone specialist from Egypt?
A Cairopractor.

What do you call two half rabbits that get together?
A rabbit "whole."

What do you call a scientist whose life is in ruins?
An archaeologist.

What do you call a room that doesn't require wallpaper or paint, doesn't have a floor to carpet or tile, and prefers a damp dark atmosphere?

A mushroom.

What do you call a person who doesn't return library books on time?

A bookkeeper.

What do you call an object that becomes more wet as it dries?

A towel.

What do you call a lion tamer who sticks his right arm in the lion's mouth?

Lefty.

What do you call a Moose after a long shower?

Bull Wrinkle.

what do you get. . . ?

What do you get when you cross a dog with an elephant?

A very nervous postman!

What do you get if you cross a cactus and a bicycle?

Flat tires!

What do you get when you cross a race horse and French fries?

Fast food.

What do you get from a pampered cow?

Spoiled milk.

What do you get when you mix poison ivy
with a four-leaf clover?
A rash of good luck.

What do you get if you cross a garden hose
and an elephant?
A jumbo jet.

What do you get if you cross a snowman
with a crocodile?
Frostbite!

What do you get when you cross a blanket
with butter?
A bed spread.

What do you get if you cross a goose with
Dracula?
A count down.

What do you get when you cross a bird, a
car, and a dog?
A flying carpet.

What do you get if you cross a chicken and an earthquake?

A bunch of scrambled eggs.

What do you get when you buy a boat at discount?

A sale boat.

What do you get if you cross a watermelon and a school bus?

A watermelon with forty-five seeds (seats).

What do you get if you cross a skunk and a boomerang?

The smell that always comes back.

What do you get if you cross Glenn Miller with dynamite?

A blast from the past.

What do you get when you have a cross between "star" and "led"?

Star-t-led.

What do you get if you cross a cow and an octopus?

A cow that can milk itself.

What do you get if you cross a groundhog and a tardy student?

Six more weeks of detention.

What do you get when you put three ducks in a box?

A box of quackers.

What do you get when you cross a parrot with a centipede?

A walkie-talkie!

What do you get if you cross a kangaroo and an iguana?

Leaping lizards.

What do you get when you cross steak knives and two rolling pins?

A set of roller-blades.

What do you get if you cross a nun and a chicken?

A pecking order!

What do you get when you practice kung fu in the forest?

Chopsticks.

What do you get when you cross a pony express horse and a kangaroo?

A horse with a built-in mail pouch.

What do you get when you drop a letter in a mud puddle?

Blackmail.

What do you get if you cross a boomerang with a Chia Pet?

A present that returns itself.

What do you get when you cross a computer and a mosquito?

Too many bytes.

What do you get if you cross a novel and a vampire?

A book that you can really sink your teeth into.

What do you get when you cross a big cat and a weed?

A dandy lion.

What do you get when you cross a rooster and a wolf?

An animal that howls when the sun rises.

What do you get when you cross a mummy with a beggar?

A bum wrap.

What do you get when you cross a reptile with a side street?

An alley-gator.

what happens when. . . ?

What happens when letters commit a crime?
They get sentenced.

What happens when you take your father's piece of pie?
You get a mad dad.

What happens when you don't clean your mirror?
It gives you a dirty look.

What happens when a juvenile delinquent falls into wet cement?
He turns into a hardened criminal.

What happens when a frog's car breaks down?

He gets toad away.

What happens when you cross a judge and a basketball referee?

You get a lot of court orders.

What happens when you throw a green stone in the red sea?

It gets wet!

What happens when a light bulb dresses up in a suit of armor?

He becomes a knight light.

What happens when you tell a duck a joke?

It quacks up.

What happens when vegetables show up late for work?

They get canned.

What happens when someone is convicted of stealing clocks?

The lawyer takes the case and the judge gives them time.

What happens when a frog's car breaks down?

He gets toad away.

What happens when a king burps?

He issues a royal pardon.

What happens when trees are scared?

They are petrified.

What happens when a jigsaw puzzle has a bad day?

He tries to pick up all the pieces.

What happens when a crossword gets confused?

He is puzzled.

what is the difference?

What's the difference between a love story
reader and a farmer?
> *One reads it and weeps; the other weeds it
> and reaps.*

What is the difference between a cat and a
comma?
> *One has the paws before the claws and the
> other has the clause before the pause.*

What is the difference between a mountain
and vitamins?
> *A mountain is hard to get up and vitamins
> are hard to go down.*

What is the difference between a computer and a car brake system?
One is designed to prevent crashes.

What is the difference between a kangaroo and a mailbox?
If you don't know, I am not sending you to mail these letters.

What is the difference between a sharp-shooter and a refreshing drink?
One hits the target and the other hits the spot.

What's the difference between a mirror and a gossip?
One reflects without talking and one talks without reflecting.

What is the difference between a student and a farmer tending his cows?
One is stocking his mind for life, while the other is minding his livestock.

What is the difference between a bird and a fly?

A bird can fly, but a fly can't bird.

What's the difference between a pear and a pearl?

The letter L.

What is the difference between a December morning and a bad boxer?

One is out cold and the other is cold out.

What is the difference between here and there?

The letter T.

What is the difference between a shiny penny and a dirty nickel?

Four cents.

What is the difference between the planet Earth and her oceans?

Earth is dirt-y and the oceans are tide-y.

What's the difference between a counterfeit dollar bill and a crazy rabbit?

> *One is bad money; the other is a mad bunny!*

What is the difference between diapers and ten dollar bills?

> *One is easier to change than the other.*

What is the difference between a dry cleaner and gardener?

> *One keeps the lawn moist and the other the laun-dry.*

what kind of. . . ?

What kind of syrup do moles put on their pancakes?
> *Molasses.*

What kind of trees always come in twos?
> *Pear (pair) trees.*

What kind of umbrella do most people carry on a rainy day?
> *A wet one.*

What kind of train can't take you to California?
> *Train of thought.*

What kind of shoe has money in it?
Cash-shew.

What kind of music is popular at hotels?
Sheet music.

What kind of beans won't grow in a garden?
Jelly beans.

What kind of food do math teachers eat?
Square meals.

What kind of lighting did Noah use for
the ark?
Floodlights.

What kind of can never requires an opener?
A pelican.

What kind of coach doesn't have wheels?
A football coach.

What kind of transportation do movie stars compete for?

The Os-car.

What kind of pigs do you find on the highway?

Road hogs.

What kind of musical instrument is found in the bathroom?

A tuba toothpaste.

What kind of screen allows things into your house instead of keeping them out?

A television screen.

What kind of vaccination does your car need?

A fuel injection.

What kind of clothing does a house wear?

Address.

What kind of cheese is made backwards?
EDAM cheese. (Made backwards is edam)

What kind of coat must be wet when you first put it on?
A coat of paint.

What kind of shoes should you wear when your house is flooded?
Pumps.

What kinds of cars go on sale in the fall of the year?
Autumn-mobiles!

What kind of shoes do the chickens wear to cross the road?
Re-bok-bok-boks.

What kind of stone can be planted in the ground to produce fruit?
A cherry stone.

What kind of paper makes you itch?
Scratch paper.

What kind of flying lessons are the worst?
Crash courses.

What kind of animal cleans the ocean?
A mermaid!

What kind of eggs does a wicked chicken lay?
Deviled eggs.

What kind of material do architects write on?
Construction paper.

What kind of running means you will have to walk?
Running out of gas.

What kind of bulbs do not require watering?
Light bulbs.

What kind of animal doesn't believe anything?
Sheep. They always say, "Bah!"

What kind of animal saves you from a bullet shot?
A duck.

What kind of flower do you have between your nose and your chin?
Tulips.

What kind of material is best for chairs?
Sat-in.

What kind of music do ghosts listen to all the time?
Haunting melodies.

What kind of fish do you find on an airplane?
Flying fish.

What kind of ears do engines have?
Engineers.

What kind of pants are the saddest?
Blue jeans.

What kind of boxer wears gloves?
A cold one.

What kind of tax is charged to hitchhikers?
Thumb tax.

What kind of medicine do sailors take for sea sickness?
Vitamin sea.

What kind of water can't freeze?
Hot water.

What kind of apple has a short temper?
A crab apple.

What kind of can never needs a can opener?
A pelican.

What kind of books do BMWs like to read?
Auto-biographies.

What kind of music does a paleontologist
listen to?
Rock.

What kind of insect do you eat to kill a cold?
A decongest-ant.

What kind of musical note can't vote?
A minor.

What kind of money do fishermen make?
Net profits.

What kind of chorus singer is the cleanest?
The soap-ranos.

What kind of invention lets you see right through a wall?
A window.

What kind of car does Mickey Mouse's wife drive?
A Minnie van.

What kind of animal is always found at base-ball games?
The bat.

What kind of music do geologists listen to?
Rock music.

What kind of nails do carpenters hate to hammer?
Fingernails.

What kind of fall knocks you out but doesn't hurt you?
Falling asleep.

What kind of chairs do geologists prefer?
Rock-ing chairs.

What kind of button will you never lose?
Your belly button.

What kind of flowers ride bicycles?
Rose petals.

What kind of ears to mountains have?
Mountaineers.

What kind of dots dance?
Polka dots.

What kind of paper is not designed for
writing?
Toilet paper.

What kind of plant do doctors prefer?
An IV.

What kind of object has four legs and two arms?

An armchair.

What kind of color will you always find on a rowboat?

Oar-ange.

What kind of food did Noah take on the ark?

Pears.

What color would the stairs of a one-story redwood house be?

No color at all. A one-story house doesn't have stairs.

What kind of bow is never tied?

A rainbow.

why, oh why

Why do people change dollars into coins?
It just makes sense (cents).

Why do people become so addicted to
fishing?
Once it hooks you, you can't get away.

Why did the lazy man want a job in a
bakery?
So he could loaf around!

Why don't the Irish ever iron their four leaf
clovers?
They don't want to press their luck.

Why is a river rich?
Because it has two banks.

Why was the broom late?
It over-swept!

Why did Sally throw a clock out the window?
Her mother told her time flies.

Why couldn't the boy go to the library?
It was already booked.

Why did the aliens cancel their tea party?
They couldn't find the flying saucers.

Why did the boy bring rope to the soccer game?
He wanted to tie up the score!

Why is a sports arena so windy?
It's full of fans.

How did Sunday win the boxing match with Monday?

Monday is a week (weak) day.

Why should you always carry a watch when crossing the desert?

It has a spring in it.

Why did Jennifer go outside with her purse open?

She was expecting some change in the weather.

Why did the muffler doze off?

He was exhausted.

Why is a crossword like a quarrel?

One word leads to another.

Why did the boss put clocks under his employees' desks?

He needed them to work overtime.

Why do cowboys ride horses?
Because the horses are too heavy to carry.

Why are garbage men so blue?
They are always down in the dumps.

Why did the golfer wear two pairs of pants?
In case he got a hole in one.

Why did the hotel hire the frog?
They needed a bellhop.

Why can't bicycles stand up on their own?
They are always two-tired (too tired).

Why did the police take away the computer's license?
It kept crashing.

Why are personal organizers so popular?
They have a date for every day of the week.

Why don't eggs tell jokes?
They will crack each other up!

Why was the doctor mad?
Because he didn't have any patience (patients).

Why are pianos difficult to get into?
The keys are on the inside.

Why is a room of married people like an empty room?
Because there isn't a single person in the room!

Why did the neighbor peek over the brick fence?
Because he couldn't see through it.

Why were Adam and Eve considered noisy neighbors?
They raised Cain.

Why didn't the banana kiss the peach?
   Because he lost appeal!

Why did the broken piano call a locksmith?
   She had lost her keys.

Why is six afraid of seven?
   Because seven eight nine.

Why couldn't the court jester take his
vitamins?
   The bottle was foolproof.

Why did the captain call the river lazy?
   It wouldn't get off its bed.

Why does a fireman wear red suspenders?
   To keep his pants from falling down.

Why are teeth afraid to visit the dentist?
   They are yellow.

Why is a thermometer the most educated thing in a scientist's office?
Because it has so many degrees.

Why is Farmer Brown famous?
Everyone knows he's outstanding in his field.

Why is hot faster than cold?
You can catch cold.

Why did the Coast Guard forbid butter and sugar in their station?
It was a lighthouse.

Why do people with colds feel so tired?
Their noses are running and their fevers are soaring.

Why can't the human head be twelve inches in size?
Then it would be a foot.

Why do the windows in a church have to be
cleaned often?

They are stained glass.

Why did the jeans break out into tears?

They felt blue.

Why was the clock thrown out of the
library?

It tocked too much.

Why do scuba divers fall backwards out of a
boat?

*If they fell forward, they'd fall into the
boat!*